SPECTRUM

Science

Grade 7

Frank Schaffer Publications®

Frank Schaffer Publications®

Spectrum is an imprint of Frank Schaffer Publications.

Send all inquiries to:
Frank Schaffer Publications
8720 Orion Place
Columbus, Ohio 43240-2111

Spectrum Science—grade 7

ISBN 0-7696-5367-7

1 2 3 4 5 6 7 8 POH 13 12 11 10 09 08

Table of Contents

Chapter 4 Earth and Space Science

Chapter 5 Science and Technology

Write your answers on the lines below.

11. Explain why language and communication are important skills for scientists to have.

   _____

12. Give examples of two different scientific disciplines, and explain how observation plays an important role in each.

   _____

   _____

13. Why was the discovery of *Homo floresiensis*, considered so important in the scientific community?

   _____

14. What does the use of fire and tools by a species indicate to scientists?

   _____

15. Describe how human activity can contribute to the extinction of plants and animals.

   _____

16. In the experiment that tested the freezing point of water, why were the student's results unreliable?

   _____

17. Is a hypothesis that has been proven incorrect still useful? Explain.

   _____

18. How did Joseph Lister use carbolic acid as an antiseptic? How did he know his efforts were successful?

   _____

   _____

19. What can a dendrochronolgist learn by examining the rings of a tree?

   _____

20. Why was the study of blue mussels and their response to Asian shore crabs of great interest to scientists?

   _____

Lesson 2.1 Everything Must Change

chemical reaction: a process that produces chemical change

One way to tell if chemical changes—and not just physical changes—are occurring is to watch for some of the following signs.

- The substance changes colors.
- Energy, in the form of heat or light, is emitted during the change.
- An additional gas or solid is produced.
- The change produces an odor.

Remember, matter and energy are never created or destroyed, they just change forms. When a chemical change occurs, all the atoms that formed the original substances still exist. They simply recombined to form new molecules in the new substances that the chemical reaction created.

What's the difference between a physical and a chemical change?

Matter changes all the time around you. Burn a log, and you end up with ash and smoke. An ice cube left in the sun melts into a pool of water. Drop a sugar cube into a glass of water, and it will slowly disappear.

The way matter changes can be either physical or chemical. Smash a glass jar and you still have glass. The matter is no longer jar-shaped, but it's still the same substance. That is a physical change. One way to determine if change is physical is to ask if the change can be reversed. For example, you can heat the broken pieces of glass until they turn to liquid, pour them into a jar-shaped mold, let it cool, and you'll have a jar again.

Physical changes often occur with increases or decreases in a substance's energy level. Remember, the three physical states of matter are solid, liquid, and gas. Matter is solid when it has the least amount of energy because its atoms and molecules are least active. As the energy level increases, the energized atoms and molecules need more room to bounce around, so the substance becomes less dense and changes from a solid to a liquid. More energy leads to more expansion, and the matter changes once again from a liquid to a gas.

Elements and substances can undergo this kind of physical change when enough energy is gained or lost. Water is a common example because we see it change states often—from solid ice to liquid water to gaseous steam. Solid metals like lead and iron undergo physical changes when they reach high enough temperatures and turn to liquid. As soon as they cool down, they become solid again.

When matter undergoes a physical change, it may look different, but at the molecular or atomic level it is still the same substance. A chemical change occurs when a substance changes into another kind of substance, and the change can't be reversed. For example, the ashes and smoke of a burnt log can't be put back together to form a piece of wood again.

Rust is another common example of a chemical change. Iron atoms exposed to air and water have a **chemical reaction** with oxygen. The atoms combine chemically to create a completely different substance—a molecule with three iron atoms and two oxygen atoms called *iron oxide*.

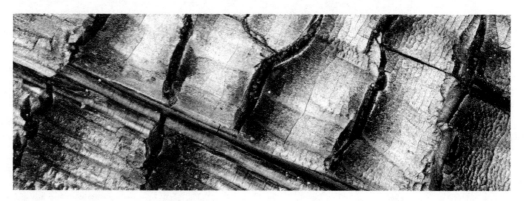

Circle the letter of the best answer to the question below.

1. In both physical and chemical changes,

   a. energy can be gained or lost.

   b. matter is created.

   c. matter is destroyed.

   d. Both a and b

Write your answers on the lines below.

2. What are three physical states of matter?

   _____   _____   _____

3. When atoms combine to form molecules, a _____ change has occurred.

Read each example of a change listed below. Decide whether the change was physical or chemical and explain how you know.

4. Fall arrives, and the leaves on the trees change colors.

   _____

5. Vinegar poured into baking soda produces a white, foaming substance that emits carbon dioxide.

   _____

6. Sugar is melted in a pan. It turns into a white liquid.

   _____

7. Sugar left on the stove too long starts to smoke and turns into a black solid.

   _____

8. A firework shot into the sky explodes into brilliant colors of light.

   _____

9. Hot asphalt poured onto flat ground cools to form a solid road surface.

   _____

10. Bread left in a bag in the dark turns green and has a strong odor.

   _____

A Common Reaction

oxidation: the process of combining chemically with oxygen

respiration: oxidation that occurs inside the cells of living organisms in order to create energy

acetic acid: the compound that gives vinegar its smell and taste

catalysts: substances that increase the speed of chemical reactions

Aluminum naturally protects itself from being destroyed by rust. A thin coating of aluminum oxide forms on the metal's surface due to oxidation. The layer prevents air and water from reaching the rest of the metal, though, so further oxidation doesn't occur.

Stainless steel—a mixture of iron, carbon, and chromium—forms a protective layer of chromium oxide due to oxidation.

Why is oxygen involved in so many chemical reactions?

Oxygen is the most abundant element in Earth's crust. It's also in the air we breathe and the water we drink. In fact, oxygen is Earth's most common element after iron, and it plays a role in many of the chemical reactions happening around—and even inside—you. Rotting fruit, rusting metal, and the carbon dioxide you exhale are all results of **oxidation**, which is oxygen molecules reacting with the molecules of other substances.

Fire is an example of very fast oxidation. When enough heat energy and oxygen molecules mix with the molecules in a fuel, they rapidly combine chemically to produce light, in the form of a flame, and heat.

Rust is an example of slow oxidation. Over time, oxygen molecules in air and water combine with iron atoms to form iron oxide molecules, better known as *rust*. Even though rust and fire are both forms of oxidation, you won't feel heat radiating from a rusting piece of metal because very little energy is involved in the reaction.

Respiration is oxidation happening inside the cells of plants and animals. Sugar and protein molecules in the cells react with oxygen and release the energy that your body needs to function.

Perform the following experiment to see oxidation in action. First, find an old copper penny. Then, get a plastic container with a lid that creates a tight seal. You'll also need some clay, a cotton ball, and vinegar.

Cover half of the copper penny with clay. Stretch the cotton ball, dip it into the vinegar, and then rub some vinegar onto the exposed copper. Place the vinegar-soaked cotton into the plastic container, and set the clay and copper on top of it. Seal the container with its lid.

After a few days, open the container. Remove the clay from the copper and you should see a difference between the two sides. The side that was covered by the clay will not have changed, but the side that was exposed to vinegar and oxygen should be darker and duller, and it might have even begun to turn green. This coloring is a layer of copper carbonate molecules formed through oxidation.

The copper will oxidize even if you don't use vinegar, but the process takes much longer. Vinegar contains **acetic acid**, and acids are **catalysts** that speed up the oxidation process.

Circle the letter of the best answer to each question below.

1. Physical traits pass from one generation to the next

   a. through genes.

   b. because of environment.

   c. according to eugenics.

   d. All of the above

2. "Nature versus nurture" can also be described as

   a. "heredity versus genetics."

   b. "DNA versus inheritance."

   c. "genes versus environment."

   d. "dominant versus submissive."

3. Which physical trait is most likely to be influenced at least partly by environment?

   a. height

   b. hair color

   c. weight

   d. eye color

Write your answers on the lines below.

4. A mother and daughter are both talented pianists. Give an inherited trait and a learned trait that would lead to this similarity.

   _____

   _____

5. How do identical twins differ from fraternal twins?

   _____

6. Why would an adopted child be a good candidate for a study of nature versus nurture?

   _____

   _____

The Ankle Bone's Connected to the Leg Bone

buffered: protected from harm

sac: a small bag that usually contains fluid

mobile: able to be moved

inflammation: the body's response to injury or infection; includes swelling and pain

Ligaments stretch across the joints from bone to bone. If you are "double jointed," you don't have extra joints, but you can bend them farther than most people.

At the base of the thumbs are saddle joints that allow your thumbs to touch your other fingers. These are the only saddle joints in your body.

While it is usually older people who suffer from arthritis, juvenile rheumatoid arthritis affects children. No one knows exactly what causes it, but research has shown that it affects the immune system—the body's system of fighting bacteria and viruses.

How do joints help your body move?

A basketball star dribbles down the court and bounds into the air for a slam dunk. A figure skater glides across the ice, leaps, and lands a triple flip-triple loop combination jump. What these athletes have in common is that they rely on the interaction of their bones, joints, and muscles.

You know that your bones provide a framework for your body and muscles power the motion, but what are joints? Joints—the points where two bones meet—keep bones in alignment and allow your skeleton to move.

The three main types of joints are classified by the amount of movement they allow. Fibrous joints do not permit any movement. Instead of being formed by a single large bone, the skull is made of bony plates that fit together like a puzzle. In between the plates is connective tissue, which is a fibrous joint.

Cartilaginous joints move just a little. The two bones that meet at a joint are **buffered** by a disc of a smooth, slightly soft substance called *cartilage*. The spine is comprised of a stack of 33 bones called *vertebrae* with 23 layers of cartilage in between. The cartilaginous joints between the vertebrae are what enable the back to bend. The bottom nine vertebrae lack cartilage and are fused in two groups to form the tailbone and the pelvis.

Synovial joints are able to move in many directions. In these joints, the ends of the bones are covered with cartilage. A **sac** of fluid surrounds the joint to provide lubrication. Three main types of synovial joints play a major role in voluntary movement. Hinge joints allow back-and-forth movement, which is similar to opening and closing a door. Elbows, knees, and fingers all have hinge joints. Pivot joints let you rotate your head. Ball-and-socket joints in the shoulders and hips are the most **mobile** joints, permitting a circular movement. In fact, the shoulder is the most flexible joint in the human body, allowing you to swing your arms in any direction.

When joints are working properly, we don't give them much thought. One problem they can develop, though, is a disease called *arthritis*. In some types of arthritis, old age and previous injuries can wear down the cartilage and cause the bones to rub against each other. This creates **inflammation** near the joint, and sufferers develop severe pain, stiffness, and exhaustion. Exercising regularly and eating a nutritious diet can help you avoid some painful joint problems and keep your body moving smoothly.

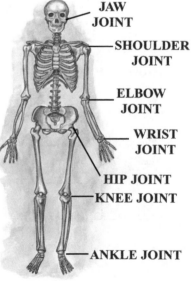

JAW JOINT

SHOULDER JOINT

ELBOW JOINT

WRIST JOINT

HIP JOINT

KNEE JOINT

ANKLE JOINT

Use the words in the box to complete the sentences below.

inflamed	ligaments	fibrous	circular

1. _____ joints, like those in your skull, do not allow any movement.

2. When a part of the body becomes injured, it may become _____.

3. A person who is double jointed has longer _____ than most people.

4. Ball-and-socket joints allow _____ movement.

Write **true** or **false** next to each statement below.

5. _____ Arthritis affects only people who are middle-aged or older.

6. _____ Saddle joints are found only in the thumbs.

7. _____ The knee joint is the most flexible joint in the human body.

8. _____ Cartilaginous joints allow less movement than synovial joints.

Write your answers on the lines below.

9. What is the purpose of joints in the human body?

    _____

10. How is a ball-and-socket joint different from a hinge joint? Give one example of each.

    _____

    _____

11. Explain why part of the spine bends and part of it does not.

    _____

12. What purpose does cartilage serve? What happens when it wears down?

    _____

    _____

13. Why would joint health be important to an athlete?

    _____

Antibiotics: Life Killing Life

compounds: two or more substances that have combined together chemically to form a new substance

exuded: oozed out gradually, as in sweat or droplets

synthetic: produced artificially

strain: a subgroup of organisms that have unique characteristics but aren't classified as a new species

Modern researchers weren't actually the first people to understand the importance of antibiotics. The Chinese used antibiotics more than 2,500 years ago. The ancient Egyptians used a mixture of lard, honey, and lint as an ointment for treating wounds. The honey contained antibacterial properties and acted as a disinfectant. The ancient Greeks used mold to treat cuts and scrapes.

Not all bacteria are harmful to the body. Probiotics are "good" bacteria found in dietary supplements or in foods like yogurt. These bacteria are naturally found in your body and can help with digestion and boost your immune system.

Where do antibiotics come from, and how do they work?

Have you ever been ill and taken antibiotics? Antibiotics are chemical **compounds** that help the body fight infection by destroying or inhibiting the growth of microorganisms like bacteria.

Modern antibiotics were discovered in France in 1897 by Ernest Duchesne, a young physician, when he found that a certain type of mold called *Penicillium* would heal wounds. He was ignored because of his youth, and his research went largely unnoticed.

In 1928, Scottish biologist Alexander Fleming rediscovered the antibiotic properties of *Penicillium*. While Fleming was studying a bacterium, he carelessly allowed some mold to grow in his petri dishes along with the bacteria. Returning from a vacation, Fleming observed that the mold **exuded** a liquid substance that killed the bacteria. Fleming named his discovery *penicillin*, but never was able to develop it for practical uses.

Ten years later, Ernst Chain and Howard Florey expanded on Fleming's work. They created a purified form of penicillin and used it to treat mice that had been infected with lethal doses of bacteria. During World War II, the team of scientists quickly applied their findings to human patients. They worked with the government to establish factories to mass produce the drug and used penicillin to save the lives of millions of soldiers. Penicillin is still one of the most widely prescribed antibiotics.

There are approximately 100 antibiotics in use today, and researchers continue to hunt for new forms. Some antibiotics are **synthetic** and are manufactured by scientists in laboratories. Others have natural sources—one of the many reasons that preserving the world's rain forests is so important. Plants found in these areas are used to make lifesaving drugs.

It is important that physicians prescribe antibiotics only when they are necessary. Antibiotic treatment may not kill every single bacterium. The bacteria that survive are resistant to that drug. Because only these resistant bacteria can survive and reproduce, a drug-resistant **strain** is created. When an antibiotic is used more frequently, drug resistance becomes more likely. Eventually, antibiotics that could once be used to cure illnesses become less effective and alternatives have to be found. Scientists must constantly search for ways to combat newer, antibiotic-resistant strains of bacteria in order to keep some of the world's most dangerous diseases under control.

Write **true** or **false** next to each statement below.

1. _____ All bacteria are harmful to the body.

2. _____ When antibiotics are used too frequently, they can become ineffective.

3. _____ Penicillin was the first modern antibiotic to be widely used.

4. _____ All antibiotics are obtained from natural sources, such as mold.

Write your answers on the lines below.

5. Explain how the modern discovery of antibiotics required scientists to build on the work of others in the field.

   _____

   _____

6. In recent years, antibacterial hand soaps have become very popular. Do you think the widespread-use of these soaps is wise? Explain your answer.

   _____

   _____

7. One problem with using pesticides to control insects on crops is that the insects can develop resistance to the chemicals. How is this similar to the overuse of antibiotics?

   _____

   _____

8. Give one example of how a group of ancient people used a version of antibiotics.

   _____

9. Why do you think there was a rush to mass produce penicillin around the time of World War II?

   _____

10. What are probiotics, and how are they used?

   _____

Nature's Talented Weavers

spinneret: a spider's organ that produces silk thread

radials: the spokes that extend from the center of a circular shape, such as a spider's web or a wheel

Trap-door spiders don't build webs, but rather use their silk thread to build small tunnel-like burrows on the ground. At the end of the tunnel, they create a small "trap door" from silk. When an insect wanders by, the spider opens the door, snags the insect, and pulls it into the tunnel to be eaten.

Scientists have found a way to produce large quantities of spider silk. They have altered the DNA of some goats so that they produce silk in their milk. Because of its strength, this goat silk should have many uses in industries where a light but strong material is needed.

How does a spider create a web?

On an early morning walk, you may have spotted a spider's web covered with dew. The tiny droplets of water can make the details of a web very visible. If you had taken a moment to examine it, you might have seen what an amazing feat of engineering a spider's web is.

Spiders produce silk from **spinneret** glands located in the abdomen. They can produce a variety of different types of silk, depending on how it will be used. For example, sticky silk captures prey, but other types of silk are used for protecting eggs or constructing a web. The silk is very light but also incredibly strong. You may have heard that a piece of steel the same thickness as a spider's thread isn't as strong. That is true. Human beings have created nothing that is as lightweight and strong as spider's silk.

The most common type of web is the circular orb web. The first step in building this type of web is for a spider to release a single thread and wait for the wind to catch it. When a breeze attaches the fine piece of silk to a nearby surface, the spider travels across this bridge, reinforcing it with another thread. It then spins more silk to create a y-shaped line suspended from the bridge.

The spider continues weaving, adding more spokes, or **radials**, to the web. Once this section of the web is complete, the spider can begin creating the spiral portion of the web that connects the radials. Within the web, the spider includes non-sticky threads that it can use during the web's construction. It will often consume these threads before construction is finished.

After about an hour's work, the spider has completed the web. The size of the web and how tightly it is woven depend upon the size of the spider and of the prey it plans to catch. Some spiders wait quietly near the center of the web for an unsuspecting insect to become trapped, while others hide out of sight. Some spin a signal thread which will vibrate when an insect has been trapped and alert the spider to its presence.

Even though creating a web uses a lot of energy, new orb webs are constructed almost every day. If an insect damages a web, the spider may try to repair it. Otherwise, the spider will often eat the silk threads and begin work on a new web the following day.

Write **true** or **false** next to each statement below.

1. _____ All spiders spin webs.

2. _____ Most orb webs are rebuilt every day.

3. _____ Spiders can produce different types of silk from their spinnerets.

4. _____ Spider silk is weak, but similar silk produced by goats is much stronger.

5. _____ A spider that catches small insects, like gnats, will have a tightly woven web.

Write your answers on the lines below.

6. Do you think that a spider web is a more efficient means of capturing prey than chasing it? Explain.

   _____

   _____

7. Explain how spiders can use vibrations to help them capture their prey.

   _____

8. How can goats create silk protein?

   _____

9. Why do you think the author of the selection calls spider webs an "amazing feat of engineering"?

   _____

   _____

Unifying Concepts and Processes

Scientists believe that the evolution of flying insects and spiders may have influenced one another. If the earliest spiders built their webs near the ground, insects that could fly would be less likely to become trapped. How do you think this affected the behavior of spiders?

   _____

   _____

Journey for Survival

migration: the seasonal journey of an animal between two locations

instinctual: driven by an inborn, unlearned behavior

temperate: pleasant; mild or moderate

dwindling: decreasing or running out

Each year in the fall, adult female eels journey from freshwater lakes and rivers to the Sargasso Sea so they can breed with the male eels that live in the coastal waters. They lay their eggs in the ocean because the eel larvae cannot survive in freshwater. When they are grown, the eels move back to the freshwater lakes and rivers.

Some birds follow a unique pattern of migration. They journey east to west to spend the winter on the coast. Other birds live at high altitudes in the mountains and avoid harsh winters by moving lower into the valleys.

Why do some animals make journeys that are thousands of miles long every year?

Have you ever watched a flock of geese heading south in the fall and wondered how they know it's time to go? The geese are following their natural instinct to migrate. **Migration** is the **instinctual** journey of an animal traveling between two locations, often seasonally.

What is the advantage of such a long journey? Some of the reasons animals migrate are to find food or a more **temperate** climate, or to give birth. Many birds travel from their northern summer homes to their southern winter homes in order to avoid harsh climates. The Arctic tern, a relative of the seagull, is an amazing migrator. Each year, terns fly more than 12,000 miles round trip between the Arctic and the Antarctic. Flying as much as 200 miles per day, the terns migrate farther than any other animal. When they arrive in Antarctica, it is December, when the summer days are long due to the tilt of the planet. As long nights return to Antarctica, the terns fly north to the Arctic summer.

Birds are not the only animals to migrate. Many species of fish migrate, returning to the exact location where they were born. Salmon swim upstream from saltwater to fresh water, struggling against the current in order to deposit and fertilize their eggs. Many salmon die after their exhausting trip.

The Serengeti wildebeests of Africa must migrate in order to survive the inhospitable climate, lack of water, **dwindling** food supply, and predators. These animals travel a circle of 500 to 1,000 miles per year as they constantly seek a fresh source of food and a safe place to give birth.

Many migrating animals actually travel the same path each cycle. But how do they know the way? Scientists believe birds are able to use the position of the sun and stars to locate their path. They also memorize the terrain of the land below them, as well as the smells and even sounds along the route. Fish, whales, and dolphins take note of the direction, speed, depth, and smell of underwater currents.

Scientists are still trying to understand all the mysteries of migration. By catching migratory animals and tagging them with electronic transmitters, scientists can track migration patterns after the animals are released. This allows them to learn more about the behaviors that drive these animals on their long journeys.

NAME _____

Circle the letter of the best answer to each question below.

1. Why do salmon migrate?

    a. to escape predators

    b. to lay their eggs

    c. to search for better sources of food

    d. because the waters where they were born become too cold in winter

2. Which of the following is not used by animals to travel the same migratory path each year?

    a. memory

    b. the position of celestial bodies

    c. the shape of the land

    d. cloud patterns

Write your answers on the lines below.

3. Explain how you think migration might affect animals in a food chain.

    _____

    _____

4. How has technology allowed scientists to study migration?

    _____

5. Why do you think some animals migrate while others are able to live in the same place year round?

    _____

6. Animals aren't the only creatures that migrate. Some groups of human beings who live off the land also migrate. Based on the selection, give two reasons they might do so.

    _____

    _____

What's Next?

Not all migrations are round-trip migrations. Do some research about nomadic migrations, irruption, and removal or one-way migrations. How do the reasons for these migrations differ from those of round-trip migrators?

Animal IQs

abstract: relating to a concept, like love or honesty, rather than something concrete, like an apple or a ball

ethologists: scientists who study animal behavior

A large brain relative to the size of an animal's body is one indication of intelligence. This ratio is the largest for human beings, followed by bottlenose dolphins and chimpanzees. Although brain size is one indicator of intelligence, scientists have found behavior to be a more useful measure.

A dolphin named *Kelly* impressed researchers in Mississippi by devising a way to get more fish. When she caught a gull passing overhead, she was rewarded with fish. She saved a fish and used it as bait to catch another gull, which meant that she was rewarded with more fish. She later taught this clever strategy to her offspring, who taught it to other dolphins at the center.

How do human beings measure intelligence in animals?

Scientists have a series of qualities they use to determine a species's intelligence—a difficult concept to measure, especially in animals. Problem-solving abilities and use of tools are two qualities scientists evaluate. Understanding language and **abstract** concepts, as well as having a sense of self-awareness, are also linked to intelligence. Because these are difficult things to measure, scientists must carefully observe behaviors and be creative with the experiments they design.

Primates have long been thought to be the most intelligent mammals besides human beings. Much of what is known about chimpanzees comes from Jane Goodall's extensive observation of them in the wild. One startling discovery she made was that chimps use tools like twigs and long grasses to fish termites from their nests. In recent years, they have also been seen making spears for hunting. Before Goodall's discoveries, scientists believed that only human beings created weapons and tools.

As the study of animal intelligence has grown, other species have also been observed making tools. In Australia, some dolphins use natural sponges to cover their snouts and protect themselves from spiny fish. Some crows use sticks to retrieve insects to eat, similar to chimpanzees.

Language and communication are also studied by **ethologists** searching for clues to animal intelligence. Both dolphins and primates have been trained in sign language and can recognize individual words, as well as the combination of a series of words in sentences. A study done with dolphins revealed that they even have some concept of mathematics. After training, they were able to identify the concept of "fewer" using display boards that showed different numbers of dots.

One of the classic tests of intelligence is to make a mark on an animal while it is asleep. When an intelligent animal is shown its reflection in a mirror, it will notice the mark and begin grooming that area of its body. This occurs in chimps, apes, and dolphins. A less intelligent animal may notice the mark but be unaware that it is seeing its reflection.

Scientists won't likely discover levels of animal intelligence approaching human levels. Instead, researchers hope to learn more about the ways in which animals are intelligent and how human beings may be able to communicate with them. This can also help scientists gain a better understanding of human intelligence and how it evolved.

Circle the letter of the best answer to each question below.

1. Both Mars and Earth

   a. have water.

   b. tilt on their axes.

   c. have atmospheres.

   d. All of the above

2. The Martian canals turned out to be

   a. filled with ice.

   b. optical illusions.

   c. canyons.

   d. marks left behind by NASA spacecraft.

3. The results of *Viking's* experiments

   a. proved that life couldn't exist in the Martian soil.

   b. proved that living organisms would be found only at the poles.

   c. couldn't be used to determine whether life did or did not exist on Mars.

   d. showed that if life did exist on Mars, it would have to exist deep underground.

Write your answers on the lines below.

4. Why would bacteria in a meteorite from Mars help explain how life arose on Earth?

   _____

   _____

5. Why are extremophiles important in studying the possibility of life on other planets?

   _____

What's Next?

NASA's *Phoenix* spacecraft is scheduled to land on the Martian surface in May of 2008. The craft will land near Mars's north pole and analyze the frozen water found there. Do some research to learn more about the *Phoenix* mission, and what scientists hope to learn about the possibilities of life on Mars.

Chapter 4

Review

Circle the letter of the best answer to each question below.

1. Which of the following is not a common effect of El Niños?

    a. droughts in Southern California

    b. flooding in Peru

    c. droughts in Indonesia

    d. warmer than usual waters along the western coastlines of the Americas

2. Which of these statements is true?

    a. All rocks are minerals.

    b. All minerals are rocks.

    c. All rocks are crystals.

    d. All minerals are crystals.

3. What characteristics of extremophiles make them valuable examples of what life might be like on another planet?

    a. They survive in conditions that are much too harsh for most other life on Earth.

    b. They have been found living on satellites that orbit Earth.

    c. Their fossilized remains have been found in meteorites.

    d. The *Viking* lander found evidence of their chemical waste in Martian soil.

Use the words in the box to complete the sentences below.

biological	plate tectonics	symmetrical	celestial	saturated	topographical

4. The movement of segments of Earth's crust, known as _____, may be one of the causes of ice ages.

5. _____ maps show terrain and ocean depths in three dimensions.

6. When the ground is completely filled with water, it is _____.

7. _____ weathering can be caused by plant roots growing in the cracks of a rock.

8. A crystal's structure consists of a repeated pattern of _____ solids.

9. The largest gravitationally-bound _____ objects are clusters.

Write your answers on the lines below.

10. Describe what an ice age is, including how long it lasts and the phases it goes through.

_____

_____

11. Are avalanches more likely to occur on steep or gentle, gradual inclines? Explain.

_____

_____

12. Give two examples of avalanche triggers.

_____   _____

13. Explain how groundwater is a part of the water cycle.

_____

_____

14. How can the water supply in an aquifer get polluted by chemicals?

_____

15. What is the difference between mechanical and chemical weathering?

_____

_____

16. Debris that was left over after the sun formed came together to form planets and other objects in the

solar system because of _____.

17. What do most of today's scientists think is the origin of Earth's moon?

_____

18. Why are scientists searching for evidence of liquid water on Mars?

_____

Lesson 5.1   Copycats

cloning: creating an exact copy of an organism

replicas: duplicates; exact copies

genetic modification: the changing of an organism by the introduction of genes it does not naturally possess

Cloning could be used to increase populations of endangered animals. Even extinct animals might be cloned if a complete, undamaged sample of the animal's DNA was found. A similar animal, a sort of foster parent, would need to be available so that the embryo could be implanted in it. For this reason, it wouldn't be possible to clone dinosaurs, even if DNA could be located.

One problem with cloning animals is that it would reduce genetic diversity. In nature, the different members of a species have different strengths, which can make the population stronger. Identical, cloned animals could be more vulnerable to being wiped out by a disease or a change in environment.

What use does science have for clones?

Although it has made quite a stir and created a lot of controversy, **cloning** is nothing new. To clone something is to create an exact copy of it. Identical twins are genetically exactly the same, but they aren't clones because one twin wasn't created from the other. Some single-celled bacteria reproduce by cloning, meaning that a cell duplicates its DNA, and the offspring are exact **replicas** of the parent organism. Even some plants reproduce by cloning.

This type of natural cloning isn't what all the controversy is about, however. For years, scientists around the world have been experimenting with ways in which animals can be cloned using the cells of an adult animal. When two parent animals reproduce under normal conditions, the offspring will have a random mixture of genes from each parent. Cloning takes away the element of chance. A clone has only one parent, and thus the exact same set of genes as that parent.

Advances in technology have given scientists the ability to determine which traits they want a generation of plants or animals to possess—a process called **genetic modification**. The advantage of this is that crops can be produced that are resistant to certain diseases or drought. Vegetables may grow especially large or have a long shelf. A breed of cow may produce extra-large quantities of milk. Cloning a genetically-modified organism would allow scientists to create large quantities of desirable animals that could save farmers and consumers lots of money.

In 1996, the first successfully cloned mammal, a sheep named *Dolly*, was born. Since that time, about a dozen other species of animals, including deer, horses, pigs, and cats, have been cloned. These animals tend to have health problems, though, and seldom reach old age.

The cloning of animals has also raised all sorts of ethical and religious questions. Is it morally okay to duplicate a living creature? If animals can be cloned, will human beings be next? What sorts of problems could this create? For example, could human beings be created to have certain desirable characteristics, such as physical beauty or exceptional athletic ability? Currently, many countries have a ban on cloning human beings because of moral concerns and worries that serious defects could result. It's likely, though, that someday there will be human clones. It may not occur in our lifetimes, but it will present future generations with many interesting issues.

Use the words in the box to complete the sentences below.

| controversial | DNA | characteristics | genetic diversity |

1. Two organisms that are exactly the same share the same _____.

2. _____ means that animals within a population have a variety of strengths.

3. Because of the many ethical issues that surround cloning, it is a _____ subject.

4. Genetically modified animals often possess _____ that farmers find valuable.

Write your answers on the lines below.

5. How are identical twins different from a clone and its parent? How are they similar?

_____

_____

6. What two main conditions are necessary for an extinct animal to be cloned?

_____

7. In theory, which would be more likely to be cloned—a prehistoric relative of the tiger or a brontosaurus? Explain your answer.

_____

8. How does genetic diversity benefit a population of animals?

_____

_____

9. What is genetic modification, and how does it play a role in the cloning of animals?

_____

Unifying Concepts and Processes

Are cloned animals really exactly like? If a human being were cloned, would he or she be an exact replica of the parent who provided the DNA? Use what you know about heredity and environment (nature versus nurture) to form a detailed response.

_____

_____

Where Art and Science Meet

pigments: dry, colored substances from nature that are ground up and mixed with water, oil, or another base to create paints

digital technology: devices, such as computers, cameras, or musical instruments, that use digital code

medium: a material or technique used by an artist

printmaking: an artistic medium that involves making multiple copies of an image

etching: the process of creating images on a metal, glass, or other type of plate through the corrosive action of an acid

corrosive: having the power to wear away by chemical action

lithography: a printing process in which a plate is treated to retain ink in the areas of the image, while the nonimage areas are made to repel ink

viscosity: the resistance of a substance to flow

"Art is born of the observation and investigation of nature."
—Cicero, ancient Roman statesman and philosopher

How do scientific discoveries impact the world of art?

Artists have always relied on science and technology to provide them with new methods of expression. Painting, for example, started with the discovery of how to extract **pigments** from nature. Tools for carving wood and stone had to be invented before anyone could begin sculpting. **Digital technology** is one of the newest means of artistic expression.

In the history of art, photography is also a relatively new artistic **medium**. It's a form of **printmaking** that uses light-sensitive chemicals. The special properties of these substances were discovered only a couple of hundred years ago, but artists soon found ways to use them creatively. Chemistry plays an important role in other forms of printmaking as well. Here are two examples of how chemical properties are used by printers.

- **Etching** was discovered about 500 years ago. An artist uses **corrosive** chemicals to etch an image into a copper plate. First, the plate is covered with a thin layer of asphalt. Then, using a sharp tool, an image is scratched into the asphalt. Anywhere a line has been made exposes the copper underneath the asphalt. The plate is submerged in a vat of strong acid, and the exposed copper gets eaten away. After a while, the plate is lifted out of the vat, the acid is rinsed off, and the asphalt is removed. The copper plate now has etched lines that echo the image that had been scratched into the asphalt. The plate is covered in ink and then wiped off, but ink remains in the etched lines. Wet paper pressed against the plate absorbs the remaining ink, and the printing process is complete.

- **Lithography** was invented around 1800. It works because of **viscosity**, or the different "thicknesses" liquids have. Viscosity is the reason that oil and water don't mix. First, an image is drawn onto a lithographic plate, usually made of limestone or aluminum. Then, a salt solution is spread across the plate. This solution gets absorbed into the plate wherever the image doesn't block it. Next, the image is wiped away and the plate is moistened with water. The water is drawn to the salty areas and away from those areas that had been protected by the image. Then, an oil-based ink is rolled across the plate. Oil and water don't mix, so the ink only sticks to the dry areas that were created by the original image. Paper pressed against the plate picks up the ink, and the printing process is complete.

Circle the letter of the best answer to each question below.

1. A copper plate that has been etched

   a. uses acid-based inks.

   b. holds ink in thin grooves that were eaten into its surface.

   c. can print only onto acid-free paper.

   d. uses asphalt instead of ink to print an image.

2. Viscosity refers to

   a. the plates used in the lithographic printing process.

   b. the acid used to etch copper plates.

   c. how easily a liquid flows.

   d. how quickly a digital device processes information.

Write your answers on the lines below.

3. What do you think would happen if you removed the copper plate from the acid bath too soon?

   _____

4. Choose any artistic medium, and then describe how a technology or scientific discovery not already mentioned in this selection influences it or makes it possible.

   _____

   _____

5. Do you think creativity is important in science as well as art? Why or why not?

   _____

   _____

What's Next?

In 2000, artist Eduardo Kac asked a laboratory to combine the genes of a rabbit with genes from a type of glowing jellyfish. Alba was the result—a genetically-modified rabbit that glows green in the dark. Many people were offended by this work and considered it to be cruel. Others believed it was a new, creative form of artistic expression using cutting-edge scientific research. What do you think?

Write your answers on the lines below.

11. Why is cloning a controversial topic?

_____

_____

12. What is one benefit to cloning animals?

_____

13. Explain both the chemical and physical changes that occur when copper is etched.

_____

_____

14. How did the railroad industry have an impact on the construction of skyscrapers?

_____

15. How are wind tunnels used in the creation of skyscrapers?

_____

16. Explain the difference in shape between a concave and convex lens and the effect each has on light waves.

_____

_____

17. What form of electromagnetism do satellites detect to measure temperatures on Earth?

_____

18. Explain how the Internet is a collaborative invention.

_____

19. After dialing a number on a cell phone, where is the first place the signal travels to?

_____

20. Explain the difference between fission and fusion.

_____

Lesson 6.1   Say Cheese

plaque: a sticky, clear film that forms on the teeth

tartar: also called *calculus*; hardened plaque found on the teeth

Don't forget to brush your tongue each time you brush your teeth. Bacteria that live on your tongue can contribute to bad breath, also known as *halitosis.*

It's fine to have an occasional sweet treat—just brush your teeth afterward, or at least rinse your mouth with water. Try to avoid soda and other sugary drinks. If you do have one, use a straw so that the sticky liquid has less contact with your teeth, and rinse with water or brush your teeth when you're done.

Chewing sugar-free gum can actually be good for dental health. It keeps the saliva flowing, which washes away the acid on your teeth.

What's the best way to keep your pearly whites clean and healthy?

As a small child, you had a set of only 20 teeth until your permanent or adult teeth came in. Today, you have 32 teeth that need to last you a lifetime. Taking good care of your teeth is simple once you establish good habits.

Plaque is a sticky, clear film that builds up on your teeth. If you've ever forgotten to brush, you know just how it feels in your mouth. Not only can plaque cause bad breath, it can also lead to cavities. When you eat food that contains sugar and starches, plaque forms on your teeth. Bacteria in your mouth digests the plaque to form an acid that eats away at your enamel—the hard, protective coating on your teeth. When this happens repeatedly, the enamel breaks down and the tooth decays.

Cavities aren't the only damage that plaque causes, either. Over time, plaque that remains on the teeth hardens into **tartar**. Tartar makes it more difficult for you to properly clean your teeth. It can also lead to gingivitis, a form of gum disease, in which the gums are painful, irritated, and may bleed. This can be more than just an annoyance. Studies have found that poor dental health is actually considered a strong risk factor for heart disease.

Flossing is as important as brushing because it removes food and plaque from the spaces in between your teeth where the toothbrush can't reach. Flossing also strengthens your gums and helps keep them healthy.

Eating well is important to the health of your teeth, just as it is for the rest of your body. Foods rich in calcium, such as dairy products, help build healthy teeth and bones, where 99% of the body's calcium is found. Vitamin D is also essential, because it allows the body to absorb calcium. It's found in fortified foods, like milk, but it doesn't occur naturally in most foods. Luckily, the body can manufacture Vitamin D itself through exposure to ultraviolet sunlight for just a few minutes a day.

Even if you take all the proper measures to have a healthy mouth, regular visits to the dentist—approximately every six months—are still necessary. A dentist will clean your teeth, removing the tartar that builds up no matter how well you brush. He or she can also check for cavities and other problems, like gum disease or oral cancer.

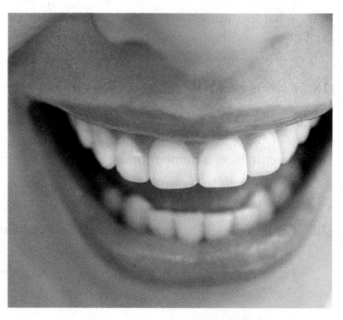

Write **true** or **false** next to each statement below.

1. _____ Human beings have more teeth as adults than they do as young children.

2. _____ Chewing any kind of gum is damaging to the health of your teeth.

3. _____ It's best to schedule a visit to the dentist once every two years.

4. _____ Brushing your tongue can help keep your breath smelling fresh.

5. _____ The human body can manufacture its own calcium and Vitamin D.

6. _____ Flossing can be a substitute for brushing your teeth.

7. _____ Plaque that is not removed from the teeth and hardens is called *tartar*.

8. _____ Gingivitis is a treatment that can prevent the formation of cavities.

Write your answers on the lines below.

9. Although it's best to avoid drinks that are high in sugar, what should you do if you have one?

_____

_____

10. Explain why both Vitamin D and calcium are necessary for the health of your teeth and bones.

_____

_____

11. What are two sources of Vitamin D?

_____

12. How do cavities form?

_____

_____

13. How does dental health relate to the health of other systems in the body?

_____

legumes: a family of protein-rich food plants that includes peas, beans, and peanuts

glucose: a form of sugar that travels through the bloodstream and provides fuel to cells

antioxidants: substances found in certain foods that can combat free radicals

free radicals: compounds that can harm living cells

Trans fatty acids are most often found in fast foods and prepackaged foods, like French fries, snack crackers, and cookies. Not only can they be harmful to brain functioning, they can also contribute to heart disease.

Some nutritious foods, like milk and fruits, contain simple carbs. Don't avoid them just because they don't have complex carbs. They have other health benefits that make them worth eating. Try to stick to whole fruits instead of fruit juices, and remember to choose low-fat milk, yogurt, and cheeses.

What's the best way to feed your brain?

Eating nutritious foods can help you stay fit and trim. Even more importantly, it can contribute to brain health. Many people don't realize that the foods they eat affect memory, mood, behavior, and thinking skills. By making certain foods a part of your diet, you can increase your brain power and help your brain achieve peak performance.

About two-thirds of the brain is composed of fats. Fatty acids make up a large part of the membranes of neurons—the nerve cells that transmit messages within the brain. Your body needs two types of essential fatty acids. Omega-3s can be found in cold-water fish, like salmon, trout, and sardines, as well as in nuts and avocados. Omega-6s are found in sunflower, corn, soy, and sesame oil, as well as in nuts, seeds, and **legumes**. The body can't manufacture these fatty acids, so you need to consume them regularly.

Amino acids, also important to brain health, are found in protein-rich foods like fish, meat, eggs, and dairy products. Your brain needs amino acids to form neurotransmitters—chemicals that can affect your moods and feelings. Neurotransmitters play a role in your ability to concentrate, feel motivated and alert, create memories, sleep well, and learn.

Just as a car needs gasoline to perform, your brain needs fuel provided by **glucose**. Have you ever skipped breakfast and found yourself unable to concentrate at school? Low blood sugar could have been responsible. Glucose is found in carbohydrates, but it's better to choose complex carbs than simple ones. Complex carbs are found in whole-grain breads, cereals, and pastas, as well as in legumes and some vegetables. They take your body longer to digest, so they release energy over a period of time. Soda and sugary foods contain simple carbs. A rush of sugar can make you briefly feel energized, but a few hours later you'll "crash" and feel even more tired.

Micronutrients, such as vitamins and minerals, are the final key to keeping your brain healthy and happy. **Antioxidants**, like vitamins E and C, are especially important in fighting **free radicals**, or harmful ions. Fruits and vegetables, seeds, nuts, whole grains, eggs, fish, lean meats, and dairy products are excellent sources of micronutrients.

Eat a nutritious and varied diet, and you'll notice the effects in your ability to think clearly, learn quickly, remember things, and feel content. What could be more important than the health of your brain?

Circle the letter of the best answer to each question below.

1. In which of the following foods are trans fats most likely to be found?

    a. scrambled eggs

    b. a chicken sandwich

    c. potato chips

    d. mashed potatoes

2. Why is it important to eat foods that are rich sources of antioxidants?

    a. They turn the sugars in simple carbs into complex carbs.

    b. They help release glucose more slowly into your body.

    c. They protect your body's cells from micronutrients.

    d. They fight free radicals, which can damage the cells in your body.

Write your answers on the lines below.

3. Look at each meal listed below. Choose the meal that is a better choice for your brain, and list three reasons why.

    Meal A: a glass of grape juice, a hamburger on a white bun, a baked potato with full-fat sour cream and cheddar cheese, and a chocolate milkshake

    Meal B: a bowl of sliced strawberries, fish tacos on a whole-grain tortilla with shredded lettuce and tomato salsa, and low-fat yogurt with chopped nuts and dried fruit

    _____

    _____

4. Give examples of three foods that contain essential fatty acids.

    _____

5. Explain why it's wise to choose complex carbohydrates over simple ones, and give an example of each.

    _____

    _____

    _____

Looking for Alternatives

alternative medicine: any form of medical treatment used instead of traditional Western medicine

immune: able to resist a disease

philosophies: systems of ideas and beliefs

complementary medicine: the combined use of Western medicine and alternative medicine, utilizing the strengths of each

China has a written history of acupuncture that is more than 2,000 years old, but tiny stone needles have been found that are at least 4,000 years old. People later used gold, silver, and bronze needles. Today's acupuncture needles are made of surgical steel.

Yoga is a health philosophy that has been around for at least 5,000 years. It comes from an ancient civilization in what are now India and Pakistan. Yoga is more than just stretching exercises; it is a whole philosophy of breathing, relaxation, nutrition, and meditation.

The federal government does not test herbal medicine as it does prescription medicine, so consumers need to be careful.

What should people look for, or look out for, in natural healing?

Alternative medicine is treatment that is different from traditional Western—meaning European and North American—health care; however, in other parts of the world, these alternative medicines are actually standard treatments. Some are complete systems of treatment that include different ideas about how the body works, herbal medicine, and the connection between the mind and the body.

Homeopathy was developed in Germany in the early 1800s. It's based on the idea that "like is cured by like." This means that if a large dose of a substance would create symptoms of an illness in a healthy person, a very small dose of it will cure a sick person of that illness. The concept behind vaccines is similar—when a person receives a very small or mild dose of a disease, the body can become **immune** to it.

Modern chiropractic medicine was first practiced in 1895, although there are records of the ancient Chinese performing spinal manipulations as long ago as 2700 B.C. Chiropractic medicine is based on the idea that illness can be the result of the spine being out of alignment, especially if it presses on nerve endings. To treat this, a doctor will perform adjustments, or quick thrusts that move the spine back into alignment.

Acupuncture is a form of traditional Chinese medicine that is thousands of years old. It's based on the theory that energy moves through invisible channels in the body. Very thin needles are inserted into the skin for 5 to 20 minutes to free blocked energy. Chinese herbal medicine is often used as a part of this treatment.

Western doctors have been hesitant to trust alternative medicines, partly because they have completely different **philosophies** about health and how the body works. In addition, alternative medicine can be hard to test scientifically. For example, acupuncture has been reported to be very effective in relieving pain, but this is difficult to prove because some people can tolerate more pain, and pain is hard to measure.

More and more people in the Western world are trying alternative healing, often for long-term diseases that don't respond to traditional medicine. Herbal medicine can be very powerful—about 25% of Western prescription medicines come from plants. Some Western doctors now practice **complementary medicine**, which is Western medicine used along with some alternative healing.

Write **true** or **false** next to each statement below.

1. _____ Herbal supplements are subject to the same tests and regulations that prescription medications are.

2. _____ Yoga is an ancient philosophy of health that involves stretching, breathing, and meditation.

3. _____ Acupuncture is a recently invented medical therapy.

4. _____ The types of medical treatments that Americans refer to as "alternative" may be traditional treatments in other parts of the world.

5. _____ Alternative forms of medicine and medical treatment are never effective.

6. _____ Anything labeled as being natural is guaranteed to be healthful.

7. _____ The use of herbs is often a part of acupuncture treatment.

Write your answers on the lines below.

8. What does the phrase *like is cured by like* mean? How does this concept apply to medicine?

_____

_____

9. Why do you think more people are willing to try alternative forms of medicine and treatment? Give at least one reason not mentioned in the selection.

_____

_____

10. What is the basis of chiropractic medicine?

_____

11. What is complementary medicine? Do you believe that it's a good choice for treatment? Explain.

_____

_____

food-borne illnesses: any sicknesses or infections caused by eating foods that contain bacteria, viruses, or toxins

At temperatures above 40°F, some types of bacteria can double in number every 20 minutes.

More than 75 million people experience **food-borne illnesses** every year, and as many as 5,000 die as a result. Salmonella is a common food-borne illness caused by bacteria in eggs and poultry. Symptoms can include nausea, diarrhea, and vomiting.

It's a good idea to keep a small fire extinguisher within reach of the stove. In case of a kitchen fire, immediately call an adult for help. If the fire is in the oven, close the door and turn off the heat. An adult can use baking soda to extinguish grease and electrical fires. If possible, he or she can also cover the fire to cut off the supply of oxygen.

What safety and health risks are hiding in your kitchen?

The kitchen can be the source of household injuries and even illness. Here are some tips to help you stay safe in the kitchen.

General Safety

- Always wash your hands before you begin preparing any food. If you touch raw meat or eggs, wash your hands again thoroughly for at least 20 seconds, using soap, warm water, and a brisk rubbing motion.

- Don't eat unbaked cookie dough. It contains raw eggs, which can be a source of salmonella bacteria.

- Leftovers should not remain unrefrigerated for more than two hours.

- All fruits and vegetables should be washed. They can be dirty, contain bacteria, and have residues of pesticides on them. For thicker-skinned produce, like potatoes, use a stiff brush to remove the dirt.

- Foods should always be thawed in the refrigerator and never left on the counter. If left out, the outside of the food may thaw (which allows bacteria to grow) while the inside is still frozen. To speed up thawing, place the food in a plastic bag and immerse it in a bowl of cold water. Change the water every half-hour until the food is thawed. Do not re-freeze unless the food has been thoroughly cooked first.

- Color isn't always a reliable indicator, so the best way to determine if meat is fully cooked is by using a meat thermometer. Ground poultry should reach a temperature of 165°F, while other ground meats should reach 160°F. Temperatures vary for other cuts of meat but can be found in cookbooks and at the USDA food safety Web site.

Microwave Safety

- Microwave foods only in microwave-safe glass and plastic containers. Plastics that aren't intended to be used in the microwave can leach chemicals into your food or even melt.

- Be careful when removing food from the microwave. Use a potholder, and watch out for steam when you uncover the food.

- Make sure that microwaved foods are heated evenly by rotating them. If you don't, certain portions of the food might not get completely cooked and any bacteria may not be killed.

Circle the letter of the best answer to the question below.

1. Human beings share more than 95 percent of the same DNA with

   a. other mammals.

   b. chimpanzees.

   c. the first life-forms that appeared on Earth.

   d. other primates.

Write your answers on the lines below.

2. Explain how scientists created proteins in the lab, and how it helps form a theory about the origins of life on Earth.

   _____

   _____

   _____

3. What do you think will be the biggest factor in determining the maximum number of human beings that can live on Earth?

   _____

   _____

4. In the past, what did people think set human beings apart from other animals?

   _____

What's Next?

Choose one of the following questions. Then, do some research to find out what kinds of work scientists are doing on the subject and whether or not they're anywhere close to finding answers.

- When will fossil fuel supplies run out, and what alternative energy source will replace them?

- Is there a limit to how long human life spans can be extended?

- We experience life in three dimensions—four if you include time—but does the universe consist of even more dimensions that we can't sense or detect?

- Will the universe continue expanding forever, or will it stop and begin collapsing?

- Why does Earth experience ice ages?

- What is the purpose of dreaming?

- Is there an upper limit to how quickly computers can do their work?

Circle the letter of the best answer to each question below.

1. In the 1500s, _____ published a groundbreaking work of mathematics and astronomy that theorized Earth and the other planets revolve around the sun.

   a. Aristarchus

   b. Alhazen

   c. Copernicus

   d. Galileo

2. Which of the following medical discoveries was made most recently?

   a. Human beings have several different blood types.

   b. DNA's structure is a twisting ladder shape called a double helix.

   c. Bacteria are tiny, single-celled organisms that can cause illness.

   d. Penicillin can be used as an antibiotic.

3. Which of the following statements about Louis Boyd is not true?

   a. She led a polar expedition in search of the missing explorer, Roald Amundsen.

   b. She earned her degree in geology before heading north to explore the polar regions.

   c. She charted the coast of Greenland and discovered an underwater mountain range.

   d. She was the first woman to fly over the North Pole.

Write your answers on the lines below.

4. What is hydroelectric power?

   _____

5. Is nuclear fission a renewable or nonrenewable energy source? Explain your answer.

   _____

   _____

6. Briefly describe Earth's location in the universe.

   _____

7. Name a device da Vinci imagined and sketched years before it was actually invented.

   _____

8. Choose a selection from this chapter to demonstrate how science is a collaborative effort in which each new discovery builds on previous work done by other scientists.

_____

_____

_____

9. How did Hippocrates begin to change the way people regarded illness?

_____

10. Explain why the grassroots element of Wangari Maathai's Green Belt Movement contributes to its success.

_____

11. The Montgolfier Brothers thought smoke was causing their balloon to rise. What is the real reason that hot air balloons rise?

_____

12. Name something that's still a mystery to scientists.

_____

Use the words in the box to complete the sentences below.

physiology deforestation	X-rays proteins	vaccines geothermal	fjords geocentric

13. Volcanoes, geysers, and hot springs are examples of _____ activity.

14. Ptolemy convincingly described a _____ model of the universe.

15. Da Vinci dissected human corpses to get a better understanding of _____.

16. _____ can produce immunity to certain diseases.

17. _____ can contribute to changes in climate, as well as water levels in rivers.

18. _____ taken by Rosalind Franklin revealed the shape of DNA.

19. As part of her research, Louise Boyd studied _____ and glacial formations.

20. DNA and _____ are essential for life on Earth.

Unifying Concepts and Processes

Possible answer: Smaller hardware has meant that cell phones can now contain games, music, and cameras, as well as have access to the Internet.

Page 103

1. b

2. a

3. It was developed so that researchers could share information and so that the military could have backup communication in case phone lines were down during an attack.

4. The earlier computers needed to be physically connected.

5. Possible answer: As computers became more affordable, more people bought them. Since more people owned computers, it made sense for companies to begin investing in developing the Internet.

6. By hacking into a user's e-mail address book and sending itself out to everyone listed

7. via telephone, fiber optics, satellites, and cable

8. hyperlink

Page 105

1. c

2. a

3. d

4. It's difficult to create enough energy to fuse two nuclei together and get the fusion chain reaction started.

5. Both types of reactors use heat to create steam that turns an electrical generator.

6. Possible answer: Fusion creates less dangerous radioactive waste, and the reactor doesn't need to contain as much fuel.

Page 106

1. d

2. b

3. d

4. c

5. false

6. true

7. false

8. false

9. false

10. true

Page 107

11. Possible answer: Some people think it's morally wrong to try to duplicate a living creature. They are also worried about what might happen if human beings are cloned one day.

12. Possible answer: Endangered animals could be cloned to increase their populations.

13. Possible answer: Acid reacts with copper molecules, causing the surface of the plate to become corroded. This corrosion creates pits and grooves in the surface that can hold ink.

Answer Key

14. It made steel and iron more available for use in construction.

15. Models of skyscrapers are built that can be tested in the tunnels to see if they can stand up to strong winds.

16. A concave lens curves inward and spreads light waves that pass through it. A convex lens is curved outward and causes light waves that pass through it to converge.

17. infrared light waves

18. Possible answer: The Internet as we know it today wasn't invented by a single person. It came about in stages, with people working together and contributing different elements to it.

19. a cell phone tower

20. Fission is the splitting of the nucleus of an unstable isotope. Fusion combines the nuclei of two atoms into a heavier nucleus.

Page 109

1. true

2. false

3. false

4. true

5. false

6. false

7. true

8. false

9. Use a straw and brush afterward or rinse with water.

10. Your body needs Vitamin D in order to absorb and use the calcium in foods.

11. fortified milk and sunlight

12. Possible answer: Bacteria react to the plaque on your teeth and form an acid that eats away at the enamel. If there is a hole in the enamel, bacteria can cause the tooth to decay.

13. People who have poor dental health have a higher risk of heart disease.

Page 111

1. c

2. d

3. Possible answer: Meal B provides berries (a source of antioxidants), fish (a source of omega-3s), and whole grains (a source of complex carbs).

4. Possible answers: fish, nuts, legumes

5. Possible answers: Complex carbs, like whole-grain cereal, are digested more slowly, so they provide the body with a steady amount of glucose over a longer period. Chocolate-chip cookies have simple carbs.

Page 113

1. false

2. true

3. false

4. true

5. false

6. false

7. true

8. Possible answer: It means that a very small dose of something that produces an illness can cure a person of the same illness. This concept is used in homeopathy and with vaccines.

9. Possible answer: The traditional treatment might not work, or they may want to try something more natural.

10. that illness can result when the spine is out of alignment

11. Complementary medicine is the combination of Western and alternative medical treatments. Answers will vary.

Page 115

Possible answers:

1. He could contaminate the tomatoes with the juices from the raw chicken.

2. The strawberries could be dirty or have pesticide residue on them and should be washed.

3. The foods shouldn't have been left unrefrigerated for more than two hours.

4. Bacteria could grow in fish defrosted at room temperature.

5. The cookie dough contains raw eggs and could cause the girls to become sick.

6. Not all plastic is microwave safe. You should never assume it is if you're not sure.

7. It can be used by an adult to put out a fire.

8. so that harmful bacteria don't grow on it

9. by measuring its internal temperature with a thermometer

Page 117

1. Because this can make the animal think that the person is its prey.

2. They shouldn't leave food or trash out, and they shouldn't let small pets or children be outside alone.

3. Possible answer: As development spreads, more roads are built, which fragments, or divides, animal habitats.

4. They are building tunnels and overpasses so that animals won't have to cross busy roads.

5. Possible answers: drought or a wildfire

6. Answers will vary.

Page 119

1. (Dead, Living) plant material doesn't usually ignite easily because it contains moisture.

2. (Fall, Winter) is one of the more likely times of year for wildfires to take place.

3. One of the most common causes of forest fires is (arson, lightning strikes).

4. Suppressing wildfires causes a(n) (decrease, increase) in the amount of fuel.

5. Wildfires tend to have long-term (benefits, harm) for plants and animals.

6. drought, high winds, lack of humidity

7. Possible answer: A backfire burns the area outside of a wildfire so that the fire can't spread. It is effective because the wildfire will not have fuel if an area has already been burned.

8. Possible answer: They clear the forest floor for new growth and keep there from being too much competition among trees for resources.

9. high winds and a lot of dry, dead wood on the forest floor

10. Answers will vary.

11. They can give firefighters information about the speed and direction a fire is moving.

Page 121

1. c

2. Possible answer: Each layer of an ice core contains air bubbles that have chemical information about a time in Earth's climate. These layers reveal thousands of years' worth of information about Earth's climate.

3. Possible answer: The ice in Antarctica is frozen fresh water.

4. Possible answer: Fewer people live in Antarctica than anywhere else on Earth, which means fewer fossil fuels or other polluting materials are used there.

Unifying Concepts and Processes

1. Earth tilts on its axis.

2. entropy

Page 123

1. a

2. b

3. It can damage them by eating away at their surfaces.

4. Their color (pink or blue) depends on the pH level of the soil.

5. Possible answer: It would cause the levels of acid rain to drop because fewer fossil fuels would be burned.

6. Alkaline soil can neutralize acid rain.

7. Possible answer: It can kill animals that make their homes in the water. It can damage plants and trees and cause people to have breathing problems.

8. Answers will vary.

Page 125

1. Possible answer: People began having more children so there were enough people to tend the crops, and the food supply was steadier so fewer people died of starvation.

2. Possible answer: They no longer needed to supply workers for tending crops, and the factories used machinery that got more work from fewer people.

3. Possible answer: Fossil fuels are burned to power farm machinery and to transport food around the world. Food shortages or distribution problems could arise and create famine.

4. Possible answer: The Chinese policy is a good way to control population growth so that there are enough resources for everyone. However, it doesn't seem right that people would lose the freedom to choose how large their families are.

Page 126

1. b

2. a

3. d

4. (Plaque, <u>Gingivitis</u>) is a form of gum disease.

5. Whole-grain cereal is an example of a (<u>complex</u>, simple) carbohydrate.

6. (Homeopathy, <u>Acupuncture</u>) is the use of very fine needles inserted in specific places around the body to free blocked energy.

7. Conditions that contribute to the spread of wildfires include (humidity, <u>drought</u>).

8. Researchers at polar stations can grow (<u>hydroponic</u>, purified) plants in order to get fresh produce.

9. A substance that has a pH of 7 is (acidic, <u>neutral</u>).

10. Earth's human population is greater than (<u>6</u>, 60) billion.

11. tartar

Page 127

12. It helps the body absorb calcium, which is needed to build strong bones and teeth.

13. They take longer to digest and don't give your body a big jolt of glucose all at once.

14. They can contribute to heart disease and stand in the way of peak brain performance.

15. They can be thawed in the refrigerator or in a bowl of cold water in the fridge. This prevents harmful bacteria from growing.

16. Possible answer: They are illnesses caused by eating foods that contain bacteria or viruses. Many can be prevented by washing your hands before you eat and after you touch raw meat and eggs.

17. Possible answer: Fragmented habitats can cause accidents for drivers and the deaths of animals crossing roads.

18. Possible answer: They allow new growth to take place, and they reduce the competition for resources in the forests.

19. Possible answer: There are nine months of polar darkness. There are no cities to produce lights or pollution.

20. Possible answer: Acid rain can kill animals and plants, and it can make human beings ill.

21. the development of agriculture and advances in medicine and health care

Page 129

1. c

2. d

3. a

4. e

5. b

6. It allowed them to stay in one place, survive harsh conditions, and cook their food.

7. Possible answer: Renewable sources, like wind, are unlimited and won't be used up. There is a limited supply of nonrenewable sources, like coal, so when they are used up, new sources will have to be found.

8. power created by bacteria that feed on a sugar solution and then produce electrons

9. It caused the use of fossil fuels to rise because the factories were large and needed sources of efficient power to function.

10. Possible answer: Wind and solar energy don't require that a fuel be burned, so they don't produce pollution.

Page 131

1. c

2. Possible answer: Earth is at the center of several concentric spheres that each contain one of the other celestial bodies, with the moon closest and the stars farthest away.

3. Possible answer: The sun is not at the center of the universe. It is the center of our solar system, but it just one of billions of stars in the Milky Way galaxy.

4. Answers will vary.

Unifying Concepts and Processes

1. Possible answer: Observation was used when early astronomers tracked the planets' and stars' movements. Copernicus used math to calculate the positions of objects in the solar system.

2. Possible answer: Copernicus used some of the calculations made by Islamic mathematicians to prove his theories. Copernicus published his results so other people could study them and learn that Earth revolves around the sun.

Page 133

1. b

2. Possible answer: His extensive knowledge of anatomy helped him paint and draw very realistic human figures.

3. He kept detailed journals with notes and drawings.

4. Answers will vary.

Unifying Concepts and Processes

Observation; Possible answer: It served him well because he was able to learn a great deal about anatomy. He also studied how birds fly, which allowed him to build his flying machines.

Page 135

1. Anesthesia

2. remedies

3. transfusions

4. Antibiotics

5. vaccine

6. He helped people begin thinking about the scientific causes of illness instead of viewing it as a punishment by the gods.

7. He dissected human bodies. His books were important because no other detailed images of human anatomy existed at that time.

8. He discovered microorganisms; Pasteur and Lister

9. It allowed the inside of the human body to be seen without surgery.

Page 137

1. Possible answers: The land was dry and there were few trees left. There was conflict between people over scarce resources. The Green Belt Movement provides women with tree seedlings to plant.

2. She believes that peace will be more likely when people don't have to compete to fulfill their basic needs.

3. Possible answers: fuel, shade, building material

4. Possible answers: They run the households, so they need fuel to cook and heat their homes.

5. Possible answer: It can cause the climate to become drier and levels of water to drop in rivers and streams.

6. It went from being fertile and wooded to dry and desert-like.

Unifying Concepts and Processes

Trees use groundwater and release it back into the atmosphere so that it remains a part of the water cycle.

Page 139

1. b

2. Possible answer: DNA is a molecule that plays a role in reproduction, so a scientist needs to know about both biology and chemistry to study DNA.

3. They showed the men that DNA has a double-helix shape.

4. Possible answer: It can do both. Competition might motivate scientists to work harder in order to be the first discoverer or inventor of something. But competition might also cause a scientist to withhold research, and sharing research is a vital part of scientific progress.

Page 141

1. c

2. b

3. Possible answer: Joseph was curious about what made sparks and smoke rise.

4. Possible answer: They had to perform experiments to see what conditions they needed for a balloon to float. They had to carefully observe the results so that they knew what they were doing right and what changes needed to be made.

5. smoke/Montgolfier gas

6. Hot air was causing the balloons to float because it is less dense than the cooler air outside the balloons.

7. It is easier to carry a propane tank in a balloon than it is to carry heavy or bulky fuel, like straw and wood.

Page 143

1. true

2. false

3. false

4. false

5. true

6. Possible answer: Once a scientist returns from an expedition, he or she has to organize and analyze the data that was collected.

7. The information in it could potentially be useful to wartime enemies.

8. Possible answer: She had an independent personality, she lived in a time when women were achieving all kinds of new freedoms, and her family's money allowed her to pursue her interests.

9. She learned from firsthand experience.

10. She discovered an underwater mountain ridge, contributed to the body of knowledge of Arctic plants and animals, and charted the coast of Greenland.

11. to see how it affected radio transmission

Page 145

1. b

2. Electricity added to the right combination of chemicals can result in the formation of proteins. If lightning struck these same chemicals in Earth's atmosphere, they might have created the first proteins that became part of the first living organisms.

3. Possible answer: finding a way to distribute food to people who can't grow it themselves

4. their use of tools

Page 146

1. c

2. b

3. b

4. energy created through the force of falling water

5. Possible answer: Nuclear fission is a nonrenewable source. Uranium-235 isotopes are used up in a reaction that forms two different isotopes of other elements.

6. Earth orbits the sun, which is a star in the Milky Way Galaxy, which is located in the Local Group of galaxies.

7. Possible answer: the helicopter

Page 147

8. Answers will vary.

9. He encouraged people to consider the idea that illness and disease have scientific causes.

10. Possible answer: The people who are most positively affected by the movement are the ones making the changes, so they have a lot of motivation.

11. Because the air inside them is less dense than the cooler air outside the balloon

12. Possible answer: the origins of life on Earth

13. geothermal

14. geocentric

15. physiology

16. Vaccines

17. Deforestation

18. X-rays

19. fjords

20. proteins

Page 148

1. invasive

2. catalysts; respiration

3. attractive

4. organelles

5. homeostasis

6. Joints

7. instinctual

8. aquifers

9. symmetrical

10. magnetic

11. complementary

12. false

13. true

14. false

15. false

16. true

Page 149

17. true

18. true

19. true

20. false

21. false

22. false

23. true

24. true

25. false

26. false

27. true

28. false

29. Possible answer: Scientists need to be able to clearly and precisely explain their ideas and discoveries.

30. Too many variables make it difficult to see why one result and not another was observed.

31. Both tree rings and ice core samples contain layers that show year-by-year climate changes spanning several decades, or even thousands of years.

32. Possible answer: An odor is produced.

33. oxidation

34. conductivity, reactivity, or malleability

Page 150

35. All things in the universe naturally move toward a state of equilibrium.

36. whether genetics or environment plays a bigger role in determining our personalities and abilities

37. Possible answer: Radio waves are longer than visible light waves. They can be used to carry signals so that information can be sent over long distances.

38. Possible answers: clear-cutting for development, acid rain

39. It causes heavy rains and flooding along the western coast of the Americas, and causes droughts in other parts of the world.

40. Mechanical weathering breaks rocks down into sand, which mixes with decomposed organic matter to form soil.

41. Minerals are crystallized forms of a single element or compound. Rocks contain two or more minerals.

42. the moon, Earth, star, galaxy, cluster

43. Possible answer: Mars has little atmospheric pressure, and it has no liquid water

44. Possible answer: Some people think it is morally or ethically wrong to duplicate a living creature.

45. convex, concave

Page 151

46. Possible answer: A thermometer contains mercury inside a thin tube. When the temperature rises, the mercury expands and moves up the tube.

47. Possible answer: salmon because it contains omega-3s and dairy products because they contain amino acids

48. Possible answer: Because there is no longer a buffer zone between wild areas and developed areas and because the animals may be looking for food

49. Wildfires can damage property or threaten the lives of people living in developments that are built in or near woodlands.

50. Possible answer: Understanding anatomy helped him paint realistic figures. As a scientist, learning about the structure of the body helped him understand how it functions.

51. The trees provide fuel, building materials, and a small income for the women. The climate becomes less dry, and the trees reduce carbon in the atmosphere.

52. c

53. h

54. g

55. d

56. j

57. a

58. e

59. f

60. i

61. b